IN THE TIME OF KNIGHTS

First published in the United States by
Hyperion Books for Children
a division of the Walt Disney Company
114 Fifth Avenue
New York, New York 10011-5690

1 3 5 7 9 10 8 6 4 2

Library of Congress Cataloging-in-Publication Data on file.

ISBN: 0-7868-0651-6

Produced by
Madison Press Books
40 Madison Avenue
Toronto, Ontario
Canada M5R 2S1

Printed in Singapore

IN THE TIME OF KNIGHTS

The real-life story of history's greatest knight

BY SHELLEY TANAKA, ILLUSTRATIONS BY GREG RUHL

Diagrams and maps by Jack McMaster,
Historical consultation by K. Corey Keeble

A HYPERION/MADISON PRESS BOOK

Prologue

1152, NEWBURY, ENGLAND

◆

he knights looked like giants to the small boy. The crunch of their heavy footsteps echoed in his ears as they dumped him in a dusty heap outside the royal tent. The entrance parted, and King Stephen came out.

"Do you know why you are here, boy?" the king asked sternly.

Six-year-old William Marshal looked up at the man towering over him. He shook his head. Stephen's men had snatched him from his family manor in the middle of the night and brought him to Newbury. The king's forces were assembled outside the town gates, readying themselves for an attack.

King Stephen went on. "You are my hostage. Your father promised to surrender Newbury Castle in exchange for your life."

William knew that the king was in a fierce battle with the Empress Matilda over who should rule England. John Marshal, William's father, had been on the king's side at first, but now he swore loyalty to Matilda. She was lucky to have him. John Marshal was known far and wide for his fearless courage, his iron heart. Even William flinched at the sight of his father's scarred face, the right eye welded shut ever since boiling lead had splashed on him while he defended a burning church against Matilda's enemies. What would such a man do when he discovered that King Stephen had kidnapped his son? Even now William's father was probably sending men to his rescue. No doubt before the day was out William would be safely back at home. Tomorrow he would throw horseshoes with his brother and tell him all about his adventures in the king's camp.

King Stephen's face darkened. "But John Marshal has broken his word. During the night he sent food, knights, and archers through the town gates. He has no intention of surrendering, and he cares nothing for your safety. Your father claims he can make more sons, and better ones, to take your place."

William didn't understand. Was this a game? He knew he was the younger son, but he still carried his father's name. He kept his eyes fixed on the distant gray hills, dotted with sheep and boulders. Where were his father's men?

"Hang the mongrel pup from the nearest oak," one of King Stephen's knights muttered in disgust.

"I say return him to his father," called out another. "Right over the town walls." The knights cheered.

The king nodded. He led the boy down to the town. Outside the walls stood the giant catapult. Its soaring timbers and padded crossbar cast long shadows across the ground.

William was spellbound by the thick sling hanging from the great beam. It looked exactly like a . . .

He turned to the king suddenly.

"Please, sir, can I try the big swing?" he said, tugging on the king's tunic and pointing at the catapult. He pushed a lock of dark hair away from his eyes with a grubby hand.

King Stephen bent his head so the knights would not see his eyes fill with tears. How could he kill such a child?

For several moments he gazed down at the boy's round face. The crowd grew silent. Then King Stephen bent, scooped up William in his arms, and turned around to head back to his camp.

Skill

◆

William looked with relief at the grand fortress overlooking the mouth of the River Seine. He was tired. It had taken him three days to walk from his father's home to the coast of England. Then there had been the stomach-churning boat trip across the English Channel to France, where the wild gray waters seemed bent on tossing passengers into the icy depths.

Now the stone castle on the cliff looked comfortingly solid to William. It belonged to his cousin, William de Tancarville, a powerful baron who ran a large, busy household full of young squires and the knights who supervised their training.

This was to be William's new home. Some boys were sent away to begin their knight's training when they were only six. But John Marshal could not be troubled to make arrangements

for his younger son until William turned thirteen, already a man. William had expected little else. By the time King Stephen had returned him to his home seven years before, he had learned all too well that he was worth nothing to his father.

It would be up to him to make his own fortune. He would become a knight, and then his real adventures would begin.

During the following months at Tancarville, William mastered the combat skills with ease. He was quick and agile on the wrestling floor. And he was one of the finest horsemen in the household. He could make the most stubborn animal turn, canter, and halt at the touch of the reins. With his long legs, he could leap into the saddle dressed in full mail without even touching the stirrups. He knew how to swing a mace, wield an ax, and shoot with a shortbow.

(Above) A fifteenth-century knight charges at a quintain, an effigy that revolved when hit and could smack a hapless knight.
(Right) William Marshal (far right) and another young would-be knight practice fighting with sword and shield.

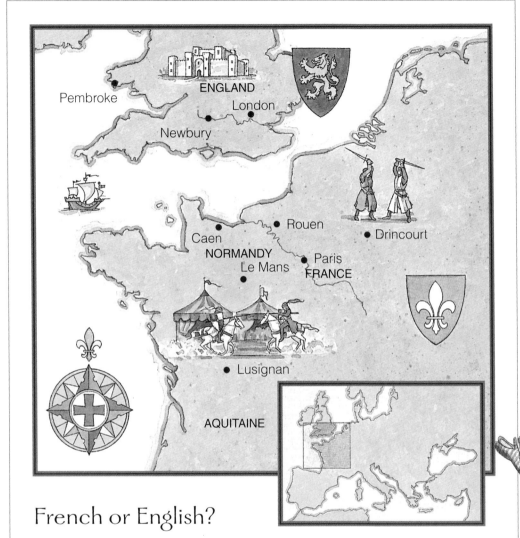

French or English?

The borders of countries in medieval Europe were very different from those of today. After the invasion of England in 1066 by the Norman duke William the Conqueror, both Normandy (a French-speaking region) and England were ruled by the same king. As part of England's nobility, William Marshal would probably have grown up speaking French, even though he was born in England. France in those days was small, largely confined to the area around Paris. To the south of it lay the powerful duchy of Aquitaine.

But there was more to being a knight than fighting. And William frustrated his tutors with his unwillingness to learn to read French, let alone Latin. He hated sitting indoors hunched over black scratchings on a page. What good would reading and writing be to him on the battlefield?

He knew that the other squires thought he would never become a knight. He could hear their sneers and insults when he passed. They said he was vain, and stupid as well. He fell asleep during Mass and could often be found after meals dozing against the sunny side of the stone keep rather than studying poetry. Worst of all, he was a pig at the table, always reaching for the meatiest joint, the choicest fruits. He never wiped his mouth before he drank from the common cup, and his nails and hands were always filthy.

Obviously he had charmed Lady de Tancarville into allowing him to ignore the finer aspects of knighthood. She was always complimenting him on his fine voice, accompanying him on the mandolin while he sang ballads he had composed himself. Even the lord ignored Marshal's failings.

He always chose his young cousin to accompany him when he hunted in the surrounding forests or hawked in the marshes that lay below the castle.

As for William, he longed only for the chance to test his skill in battle. But until he was proclaimed a knight, he would not be allowed to actually fight. Instead he would practice on wooden dummies inside the castle walls, comb the horses, polish spears, and watch the real action pass him by.

The months at Tancarville Castle dragged into years, and each day was filled with one thought only. When would he end his apprenticeship and be given a chance to show his worth? When would he finally become a knight?

The Feudal World

In the Middle Ages, peasants labored for their feudal lord in exchange for protection and the right to work and live on the land. Each lord in turn served a higher master, all the way up to the king. (Some great feudal lords, however, were almost as powerful as the king.)

The right to own land was a rare privilege, and property, castles, and titles usually passed down only to the eldest son. Noble families arranged for their daughters to marry into other noble families or to enter convents. For younger sons, becoming a knight was one of the few ways to gain money or status.

(Above left) Peasants harvest a field, watched over by the reeve, the supervisor who worked for the feudal lord. (Above right) The lord and his family at dinner. (Below) The central tower, or keep, of Dover Castle in England. Built in 1180 by King Henry II, it is a finely preserved example of a great feudal castle.

◆

illiam walked across the courtyard to the castle steps at Drincourt. The garrison was filled with knights, some leaning forward in their saddles, others standing with arms folded as they muttered and joked among themselves. They paid little attention to the solemn twenty-one-year-old who was about to become a knight. Even the horses seemed impatient for the quick ceremony to be over, their hooves restless as they shuffled and snorted.

It was hardly the way William had pictured the most important day of his life. He had always imagined himself carefully bathing the night before, putting on the plain white tunic to symbolize his purity. He saw himself spending the night in the abbey, kneeling over his sword as he dedicated himself to his God, his king, and his lord. Then the solemn moment itself, the presentation of the golden spurs and armor, the precious sword and the dubbing, perhaps by the king himself. And finally a full week of feasting and festivities, as relatives gathered to celebrate.

There would be no such family gathering for him. His father had died two years before, leaving all his lands, money, and titles to the eldest son, John. William did not even go to the funeral. He felt he owed his father nothing.

His future lay here in Normandy, where there were battles to be fought. Henry II was the English king now, and his lands were being threatened by France. De Tancarville had been called to Drincourt to defend the Normandy border with every knight he could muster. What better time to initiate his young cousin?

William approached his cousin, who was waiting at the steps, surrounded by his attendant knights. De Tancarville presented him with a new cloak and a horse. Then he reached over to gird the belt and sword to his side.

William knelt and bowed his head.

"Do you wish to become my man?" de Tancarville said.

"I wish it, and I promise that I will be loyal to my lord and give him my homage in good faith."

"Be worthy, then. I make you a knight," de Tancarville said, and he brought down his own sword heavily on William's shoulder.

William did not flinch, though the blow nearly knocked him off his knees. He stood and raised his head, and the other knights cheered.

(Above) A prince dubs two knights in this illustration from the 1400s. Once knighted, they served only him.

"I Dub Thee"

The knighting ceremonies depicted in movies often feature a fair maiden gently tapping a knight with a light sword, as Queen Elizabeth II of Great Britain does today when knighting someone. But in William Marshal's day, the tap was a real blow from a heavy sword. It was given by the knight's lord, often the king himself. Dubbing bound the knight to serve his master, and was regarded as a very serious matter. Knights often kept an all-night vigil in a chapel before the ceremony. Some took a special bath beforehand to purify themselves. After being dubbed, a new knight often had his sword buckled on by his master, and was given a new pair of spurs.

The next day came the news that French soldiers had invaded Normandy, burning every town and village in their path. And they were heading straight for Drincourt.

William mounted his horse quickly and turned toward the outskirts of town to meet the enemy forces. He was eager for battle as he pushed his way to the front of the party of knights.

"William, don't be so impatient," called de Tancarville. "Let the knights go first."

Embarrassed, William pulled back to let others pass, but only for a moment. He was a knight now. And he would take his place at the front.

The enemy party was riding toward them at a full gallop, right into the streets of the town. He spurred on his horse and rode to meet them, his knees rigid as he pointed his lance directly at the enemy shield, just as he had practiced so often.

The first impact broke his lance. William threw the wooden shaft to the ground and grabbed his sword. The streets were narrow, giving the horses little room to maneuver. From the windows and doorways the townspeople cheered on the Norman forces. To William, the cheers seemed meant for him, and he pushed into the fray.

He never saw the thirteen knights who came at him from a side alley. A heavy iron hook caught him on the shoulder, ripping the links of his mail and gouging into his chest through his leather vest. He held his seat, but suddenly his horse received a spear point to the neck, and he felt the animal shudder and buckle beneath him.

William was pulled off the saddle, the hook still caught in his mail. He tried to gain his footing on the road, now slippery with the blood from his own horse. He cut his way free. Then he headed back into the heart of the battle, swinging his sword with all his might.

By the end of the day, de Tancarville and his Norman

A medieval battle depicting a king surrounded by his knights. These battles were wild affairs, usually fought at close quarters with slashing swords.

troops had withstood four charges on Drincourt, but they had held their ground and finally driven back the enemy.

That night, there was a huge feast to celebrate the victory. The grateful townspeople brought food and wine to feed the defending army, and the knights ate heartily.

William was proud to take his place among them, and he wore his torn vest like a trophy. He deserved to celebrate. He had fought honorably and bravely.

The voices grew louder as the evening wore on, and the knights took turns reliving every parry, every hostage and horse that had been taken.

William was just about to boast about the iron hook, about how he had fended off thirteen enemy knights. Suddenly the Earl of Essex, one of the leaders of the defending army, stood and raised his cup to him.

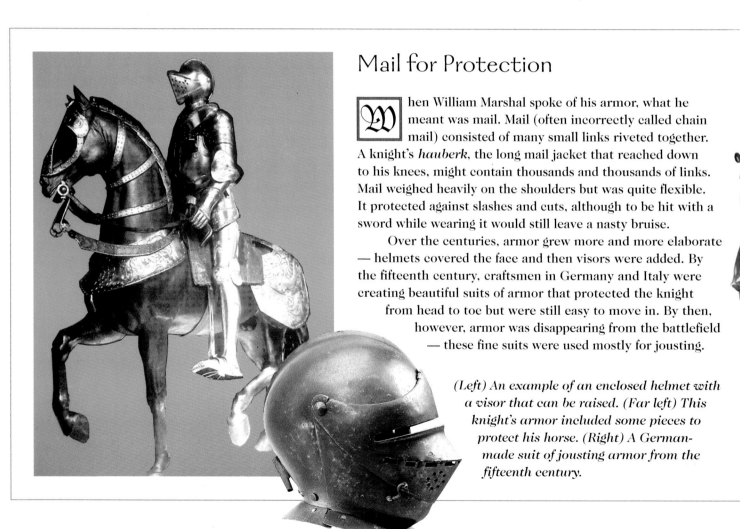

Mail for Protection

When William Marshal spoke of his armor, what he meant was mail. Mail (often incorrectly called chain mail) consisted of many small links riveted together. A knight's *hauberk*, the long mail jacket that reached down to his knees, might contain thousands and thousands of links. Mail weighed heavily on the shoulders but was quite flexible. It protected against slashes and cuts, although to be hit with a sword while wearing it would still leave a nasty bruise.

Over the centuries, armor grew more and more elaborate — helmets covered the face and then visors were added. By the fifteenth century, craftsmen in Germany and Italy were creating beautiful suits of armor that protected the knight from head to toe but were still easy to move in. By then, however, armor was disappearing from the battlefield — these fine suits were used mostly for jousting.

(Left) An example of an enclosed helmet with a visor that can be raised. (Far left) This knight's armor included some pieces to protect his horse. (Right) A German-made suit of jousting armor from the fifteenth century.

"Well, young Marshal, you've done extremely well today, we hear. What say you honor me with a little gift, just for friendship's sake?"

William laughed, but he was puzzled. "What gift?"

The earl's eyes were wide with fake astonishment. "Surely you must have gained some spoils. Can you not part with something small? Perhaps a saddle or bridle from one of your horses. I expect you took at least forty today, did you not?"

"I have nothing to give," William protested, his smile fading. "I even lost my own horse."

The knights burst out laughing. William's face grew crimson. He had helped to save a town for his king, but he had absolutely nothing to show for it. No hostages, no horses, no armor.

A true knight did not emerge from combat with nothing. He knew that now. And he vowed he would never come away empty-handed again.

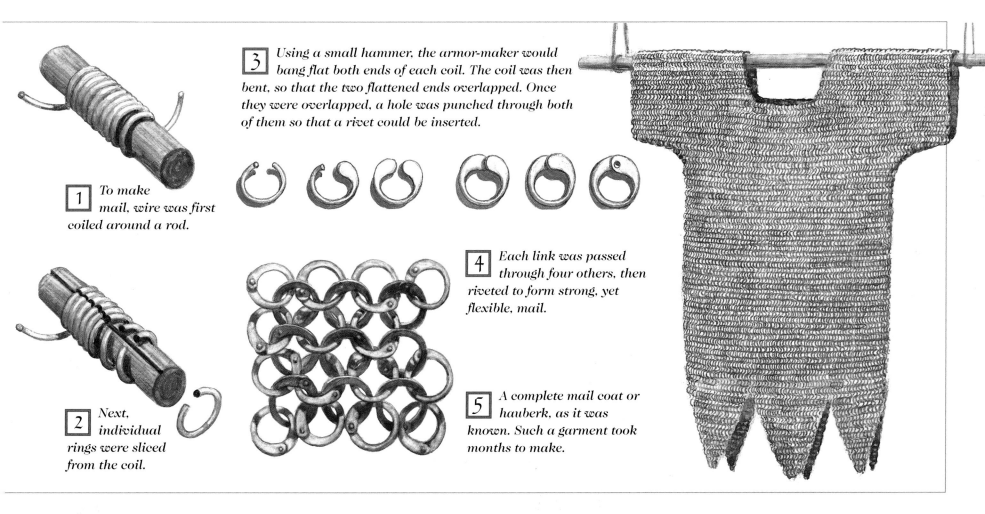

3 *Using a small hammer, the armor-maker would bang flat both ends of each coil. The coil was then bent, so that the two flattened ends overlapped. Once they were overlapped, a hole was punched through both of them so that a rivet could be inserted.*

1 *To make mail, wire was first coiled around a rod.*

2 *Next, individual rings were sliced from the coil.*

4 *Each link was passed through four others, then riveted to form strong, yet flexible, mail.*

5 *A complete mail coat or hauberk, as it was known. Such a garment took months to make.*

Courage

November 1167, Le Mans, Normandy

◆

e Mans was a carnival. The streets were crowded with acrobats, fortune-tellers, merchants, and visitors. Tents dotted the countryside as hundreds of people poured into town for one of the last tournaments of the season. Horse dealers came from as far away as Spain and Lombardy. The forges rang all night long as armorers made last-minute repairs, and knights and squires polished armor and inspected weapons and harnesses.

William felt the familiar heaviness of the mail on his shoulders as his squire helped him dress. Hauberk, leggings, hood, helmet, iron boots — with each added weight he grew bigger, stronger.

His mood soared for the first time in months. De Tancarville had called him to Le Mans to fight under his banner. Knights from all over France and England were attending.

For William, the offer had not come a moment too soon. Since his noisy victory at Drincourt, France and England had declared peace. The people had buried their dead and cleaned up their streets, and life had returned to normal.

But peace was a poor state of affairs for a knight. With no battles to fight, de Tancarville had decided to reduce his household. Before long, William had found himself wandering the countryside with no home, no employment, and no decent horse. He had had to sell his precious knight's cloak to buy a swaybacked mare to carry his armor and baggage. A good warhorse was far beyond his means, and a knight without a charger was really no knight at all. He could not enter tournaments, and without the tournaments he had no hope of gaining goods or ransoms.

In his bleakest moments, he had even considered returning to England to live with his older brother. Many young men did this. Hearth sons, they were called. But William considered it a pathetic fate for a man, living like a child under his brother's roof without land, house, or prospects for marriage.

Then, just when things had looked darkest, he received de Tancarville's offer to rejoin him. His cousin had even promised

Medieval Tournaments

Tournaments gave knights a chance to show off their skills, and practice the techniques they needed in war. They were also a way to get rich. If one knight captured another, he could keep his armor and horse and hold him for ransom. Tournaments in William's day were wild free-for-alls, with two sets of knights battling each other with swords in an open field. Sometimes, rather than mass battles, called melées, knights jousted with lances one-on-one. Over time, these contests became more orderly. Knights began using blunted swords and lances, melées were held in enclosed areas, and jousting gave way to "tilting," where a barrier called a tilt separated the two knights to stop collisions. Tournaments were sport, but knights could be wounded, even killed.

(Top) Before an audience of ladies, a knight is knocked off his horse.
(Left) A herald plays a trumpet to announce a tournament. (Above) In this scene from a much later era, two knights, separated by a "tilt," charge one another.

18

to supply him with a new horse.

William approached the beast now, shaking his head in dismay. No doubt this was some cruel joke. The stallion was practically wild, its flanks scarred from the bite of the spurs that had failed to tame it. William had to use every ounce of his strength just to mount the animal and hold it steady.

The townspeople crowded around the edges of the meadow as the knights took their places. William's charger snorted restlessly beneath him. His shield, like forty others, bore the colors of de Tancarville. He stood in the stirrups and braced himself against the back of the saddle. His lance was wedged firmly under his arm, its shaft just inches away from his horse's left ear.

William eyed the opposing knights at the far end of the huge field. He noticed one, Philip de Valogne, flying the blue-and-white colors of the King of Scotland. Philip's armor caught the sun as he strutted about like a peacock.

The trumpets sounded. A cry rang out — "Let them go!" — and the crowd cheered wildly. William's horse reared as he dug in his heels and set off at a full gallop.

William charged, his eyes locked on that blue-and-white banner as it grew larger and closer. His lance met the knight's shield and shattered, sending wooden splinters flying like darts. William tossed the broken shaft to the ground and yanked the reins hard, pulling his horse around. With his free hand, he reached out and grabbed the bridle of Philip's horse. In the churning cloud of dust and clods of

A Knight and His Horses

A knight needed several horses. For day-to-day use, he had a horse known as a *palfrey*, which he used strictly for transportation. To carry his possessions, including his armor, helmet, and arms when he wasn't using them, he needed a packhorse. But most important was his warhorse, known as a *destrier*. This was a large and powerful animal, whose speed and size added extra force to a lance's impact or a sword's blow.

earth, he dragged the horse to the edge of the field.

William pulled his captive roughly to him.

"Do you submit?" he cried, his face inches away from Philip's. Philip nodded and promised to pay his ransom.

William grabbed Philip's lance and headed back into the fray. All around him knights met in a clash of wood, metal, and horseflesh. He saw a man being dragged across the field with his foot caught in the stirrup. Screams came from below as another was unseated and trampled.

His second target didn't even see him coming — the man was blindsided by a blow so hard that his foot flew out of the stirrup. The knight, astride a splendid Lombardy warhorse, galloped to the open end of the field. William took off in pursuit.

The chase took them over farm fields and vineyards, ripping apart bare stocks as William gained ground.

The knight could ride — William would give him that. The horse flew through a village, scattering hay mows, trampling chickens. A child was pulled out of the way just in time. Some villagers shook their fists in anger. Others slammed their doors. Still others came out and cheered loudly.

In the village, William rode alongside the knight. With a

(Above) An illustration of a tournament, held on London Bridge in 1390. (Opposite) Two knights fight one-on-one in a fifteenth-century tournament.

mighty blow, he swiped him from the side. The man could not regain his footing in the stirrup, and he slowly crumpled to the ground. By the time he looked up, William was aiming his sword point at the man's throat.

The knight, defeated, went down on one knee.

William had not even made it all the way back to the field when the pack of knights came out of nowhere. There were five of them, their armor shining, their banners clean. They were clearly coming fresh to the fray, waiting for exhaustion to take its toll on the others, looking for a knight worth taking.

The first knight charged. William grabbed the oncoming lance and pushed it wide. With a cry, three others came at him, and again he fought them off, unhorsing two. Then the last knight rode in and seized him around the neck, trying to pull him off his horse.

With a fierce thwack, William forced the man back, but as he did, his own helmet twisted around on his head. Unable to breathe, blind, William fumbled with his headgear while his sword arm continued to swing.

When he finally pulled off his helmet, choking and panting for air, his attackers had disappeared, but his sword was covered with blood.

The Rules of Heraldry

In the same way that modern sports teams have uniforms to help fans identify them, knights had bright regalia that let them quickly tell friend from foe. The patterns knights wore on their coats of arms were quite simple. They used a limited set of colors, divided into tinctures and metals. Gold and silver, often represented by yellow and white, were metals. The tinctures were red, blue, black, and green. In a coat of arms, metals could only touch tinctures, and vice versa. So if your symbol was a red lion, it could only appear on a white or yellow background or be trimmed with either of those two colors. These rules seem strange, but they guaranteed strongly contrasting coats of arms, which made for easy identification.

Sunset finally brought an end to the tournament. William pulled off his armor, caked with blood and mud. He pulled a splinter from a broken lance from his left temple. There was a deep gash above his ear and bruises on his neck. His left hand was badly cut.

That night, the streets were filled with candlelit tables heavy with food and drink. The dishes jumped on the tabletop as William pounded out the measures for the dance. His blood still pumped with the memories of the day's battle and chase.

A sudden movement in a side alley caught his glance. It was a man, a thief, quietly stealing a horse — the Lombardy stallion, William's prize.

William didn't hesitate. With a roar he leaped to his feet. He ran up to the man and struck him on the side of the head with such force that one of the man's eyes was knocked out of its socket.

William was satisfied. Stealing a horse was a hanging offense, but perhaps an eye was payment enough.

A fourteenth-century lady presents a knight with a helmet displaying a heraldic device of three stars. His horse wears the same pattern on its cloth coat, known as a caparison.

Back at the table, voices grew louder and tempers flared. A bench was knocked over as two knights settled an argument with their fists.

William left the boasting to others. There was no doubt he was the man of the match. Word had spread quickly about his impossible strength, his brave stand against five knights, the prisoners, horses, and equipment he had taken. Philip de Valogne had turned out to be a wealthy courtier of the King of Scotland, and he had brought an especially fat ransom.

William knew he had finally found a way to make his mark. This younger son, cut off from his father's lands, title, and favor, was a fighter, and a courageous one.

And how he loved it — the feel of his own strength as he unhorsed the enemy, the pain of a blow bravely suffered. Most of all, he loved to win. To bring an opponent to his knees, to walk away with fine horses and ransoms amid the cheering of the crowd. Could there be anything better?

Loyalty

◆

illiam watched Queen Eleanor riding ahead, her posture erect and regal even in sidesaddle. It was said that she rode astride as well as any man. William had heard she had often chosen to do so when she had accompanied Louis VII, her former husband, all the way to the Holy Land.

William could well believe it. Eleanor of Aquitaine was the wealthiest woman in Europe, and she had a will of iron and a mind of her own. When she failed to produce a son, the French king divorced her. Six weeks later, she married Henry II, King of England, and quickly bore him three boys in five years — out of sheer spite, William had no doubt.

William scanned the forest on either side. It was the winter break of the tournament season, and he had agreed to help his Uncle Patrick, the Earl of Salisbury, escort the queen to her newly seized castle in Lusignan.

As they rode alongside the steep cliff beneath the castle, they heard an approaching party on horseback. William and his uncle stood firm while the queen fled to safety.

It was the Lusignan brothers and their men, all armed for war.

"As you can see, you have us outnumbered," Patrick said. "In the name of a fair fight, at least allow us to arm ourselves."

Geoffrey of Lusignan nodded. But as Patrick turned to order his squire to fetch his mail and shield, one of the Lusignan knights plunged his sword into the earl's back. William watched in horror as his uncle slumped forward, dead.

William had never felt such rage. Bareheaded, he rode into the thick of the enemy party, thrashing his sword in a blind fury. He managed to kill six of their horses. But he was terribly outnumbered. He held them off until a blow from a spear cut down his horse.

Still he continued to defend himself on foot. Backed against a hedge, he fought like a wild boar attacked by a pack of dogs, screaming curses and threats.

A white-hot pain suddenly cut through his right leg. Looking down, William saw the point of a sword poking through the front of his thigh. A knight had made his way around the hedge and cut him down from behind.

William crumpled to the ground.

One of the Lusignan knights stepped forward to finish the

Eleanor of Aquitaine

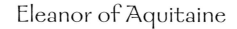

J n 1137, when Eleanor was fifteen, she inherited the duchy of Aquitaine, which at that time was bigger than France. That same year, she was married to Louis, the heir to the French throne, and a month later, when his father died, she became Queen of France. Headstrong and ambitious, Eleanor accompanied her husband on horseback to the Holy Land. She bore him no sons, however, and so he arranged to have their marriage annulled in 1154.

Six weeks later, she married Henry II and became Queen of England. She gave him five sons, two of whom became kings.

In addition to being rich and powerful, Eleanor was a patron of the arts. She greatly encouraged the troubadours, the romantic poets of her time, and she was interested in the legends of King Arthur, which promoted the ideals of knighthood. She died in 1204 at what was then the very old age of eighty-two.

(Above) Eleanor's two husbands, Louis VII of France and Henry II of England, are both shown here, bidding farewell to a bishop. (Left) Eleanor's tomb in the Abbey of Fontevrault in France has the only likeness of her made by people who saw her when she was alive. (Right) Working from this effigy, an artist created a lifelike portrait of Eleanor.

job, but Geoffrey stopped him. "This is the famous Marshal, a great fighter. He's a prize worth a fine ransom." They picked him up like a carcass of meat and flung him over the back of a mare. The blood from his wound left a trail in the dirt as they rode away.

For days they carted him from place to place, afraid that the queen's men would attempt a rescue. They treated him badly, hoping to gain a ransom more quickly. Soon William's wound was open and oozing. He tried to bind it with the straps from his leggings, but all his clothes were filthy and blood-soaked. His captors would give him no clean bandages, and his leg grew hot and swollen. He knew if he could not treat his wound soon, he would lose the leg, and probably his life.

One night, as he lay imprisoned in one of the Lusignan strongholds, a woman from the village came to the door and handed him a loaf of bread. William took it. Then he looked at the loaf more closely. It had been cut in half, the inside hollowed out. And within the hollow lay a carefully wrapped roll of clean bandages.

(Above) A wax impression of the royal seal of Henry II, showing him with a sword in one hand and a bird perched on the other. (Right) Henry II wearing his coronation robes.

Who Were the Troubadours?

Often young men of high birth, troubadours earned their living reciting or singing poetry. The first troubadours appeared in the southern parts of Europe, where life was a little easier and more settled. Eleanor of Aquitaine was a great fan, and she helped spread their songs and poems north. The pop stars of their day, the troubadours usually sang about romantic love. The ideal these songs presented, of a man pledging himself to serve a high-born lady, was one that many knights tried to follow.

(Above) An ivory carving depicting troubadours. (Left) A troubadour performs at court before the king and queen. (Below) Another entertains Queen Blanche of Spain — Eleanor of Aquitaine's granddaughter.

Queen Eleanor had never seen a knight like William Marshal. To stand and fight in the name of your queen and your uncle, even when so wildly outnumbered? She had never witnessed such bravery, such loyalty.

Eleanor paid a handsome ransom for William's release. Then she bestowed on him an even greater honor. The finest knight in the land was to raise another like him. He was to teach the knightly arts to her eldest son, Prince Henry. William had never dreamed he could be raised to such heights. He moved into the royal house-

Henry II serves his son at table after the young prince was crowned King of England in 1170. Although Henry promised his son that the two of them would be co-rulers, young Henry became a king in name only. His father kept the real power for himself.

hold to become protector of the fifteen-year-old boy who would one day be king.

William taught Henry to ride and handle arms. Sometimes he thought he saw in the boy a knight much like himself. The lad was tall, handsome, generous, charming, and ambitious. He loved the tournaments, where he would ride headlong into the fray without considering the dangers. William often found himself watching the young man's back or even rescuing him outright from his captors. Most of all, young Henry loved to win.

Yet William could see that the prince did not have what he wanted most. He longed to be independent, to rule his own domain. His father, King Henry II, was generous with titles, lands, and money, but he refused to give his heir any real power. The king was a bully with a fearsome temper, given to smashing furniture when he was crossed.

Eventually young Henry and his brothers tried to take power from their father by force. During these rebellions, many of the prince's knights left his household to pledge their loyalty to the king. But William stood by the young man.

He knew what it was like to be betrayed by a father. He would not abandon his charge.

As the years passed, William continued to do what he did best. He fought in tournaments, raising ransoms on as many as ten knights in a day. With each win, his reputation soared even higher. Young Henry cheered him on. The ransoms were sorely needed, for the prince loved to spend money — on food and drink, on horses, hired soldiers, tournaments, and the hunt. His debts grew, so that even William's considerable winnings were not enough to pay them.

But William loved the young man, for his strengths and his weaknesses, the way a father should love a son. He was so devoted that he forgot to watch out for himself. He didn't notice that he had few friends at court, that the other household barons and knights were angry at his closeness to the prince. William had seen jealousy at work among the squires at Tancarville. But in the household of a future king, it was especially dangerous.

CHRISTMAS 1182, CAEN, NORMANDY

◆

The accusations began as whispers in the castle corridors. They said that William Marshal was a mere Englishman, not even a Norman. He had no right to such a favored place in the royal household. He was an illiterate boor who was leading the prince down a reckless path, encouraging rebellion against the king. And he was arrogant, seeking his own glory before all else. Wasn't the prince himself now riding under Marshal's green-and-gold banner? Tournament heralds were even heard to rally crowds with the cry of "God help the Marshal!" instead of "God help the king!" It was an outrage.

But the worst thing, the gossips claimed, was that William Marshal and the prince's wife, Margaret, were lovers. And that was an act of treason, for which the penalty was banishment, imprisonment, or worse. Everyone knew what had happened when the Count of Flanders discovered that one of his knights had betrayed him with his wife. The culprit was beaten by the palace butchers and hung head down in a sewer until he suffocated.

In the end the prince believed the rumors, and William knew he had to defend his honor. He appeared before the royal court and demanded to be heard.

"Sire," he said to the young prince, "I have been accused of treason. Let those who charge me come forward. I will take on the three strongest, one each day. If I am defeated by any one of them, you can hang me."

But young Henry refused to listen, and none of William's enemies would take up the challenge. "Then let any finger be cut off my right hand before I do battle," William begged. "I will still stand by the result."

Still no one came forward, and the prince was unmoved. William was to leave his court and never return.

Was There a Real King Arthur?

King Arthur and his Knights of the Round Table were said to be the bravest, kindest, most devout warriors of all. Mortally wounded defending his kingdom against the Saxon invaders, Arthur was believed to have been carried away to a mystic island called Avalon. The real King Arthur was probably a sixth-century war leader who fought for the ancient British kingdoms against the Saxons then conquering England. Over time, people repeated stories about him, which grew more and more fanciful. In 1136, not long before

William Marshal's birth, a writer named Geoffrey of Monmouth wrote down many of these stories in a book called *Historia Regum Britannum* (the History of the British Kings). It caused a sensation. Real-life knights saw in Arthur and his followers an example of how they should behave. Geoffrey of Monmouth's account was followed by many other tales of knights, stories that came to be called romances.

(Left) King Arthur with his wife, Queen Guinevere, and some of their knights. (Above) As Arthur lies mortally wounded, a hand rises from the waters to take back his magic sword, Excalibur.

31

JUNE 1183, MARTEL, FRANCE

◆

After William left the prince's household, the counts and dukes of Europe begged for the services of the foremost knight in the land. They sent offers of money, lands, titles, their daughters' hands in marriage. But William had sworn his loyalty to the house of Henry. He would serve no other.

It didn't take young Henry long to realize that he badly missed the man who had been his guide and friend for so many years. He was involved in a new battle against his father, and he needed his best knight. William did not hesitate when the word came. After a long journey, he arrived at the castle and was hurriedly taken to the prince.

He scarcely recognized the young man. Henry was lying in bed, tossing with fever. His lips were cracked and white; his skin hung on his bones. The prince was dying. He would never be a threat to his father again.

He called William to him. He asked him to beg the king to forgive him. Then he had one final request.

"Marshal," he whispered weakly, "I know now that you have always been loyal to me. Promise you will carry my cross to the Holy Sepulcher so I can fulfill my vow to God."

William nodded. He understood. In his battle for power, his desire to prove his worth to himself and his father, young Henry had never fulfilled the most important mission of all. He had failed to go to the Holy Land to prove his service to God.

It was up to William Marshal to act for the prince even after his death. He assumed responsibility for the young man's debts. He arranged for the body to be prepared for burial. He rode with the coffin to the grave.

And then he went to see the king. He told him that his son had endured his final illness bravely, though he had been in great pain. He described how the prince had begged for his father's forgiveness.

The old king heard all this with stone-faced calm. But when he heard about young Henry's unpaid debts, tears suddenly came to his eyes. "It's true my son has cost me a great deal," he said sadly. "I only wish that he had lived to cost me even more."

Exhausted with sorrow, William now turned his eyes to the east. He had proven his loyalty to his liege lord, but there was one last task to fulfill.

(Above) A knight receives a blessed crucifix from a monk before departing for the Holy Land. (Opposite) William Marshal promises a dying Prince Henry that he will take the prince's cross (a Crusader's robe with a cross on it) to Jerusalem.

Service

1184, THE HOLY LAND

◆

The air was different here, William thought, as he looked out from the deck of the merchant ship leaving Marseilles. The Mediterranean was azure blue, the breezes warm and soft. Sailing here was so unlike the English Channel crossing from England to Normandy, where a knight had to be assigned to hold the king's head steady during a particularly stormy voyage.

Now the sun shone like a blessing on William's mission. Young Henry's robe was safely strapped to his back. Soon William would place it before the Holy Sepulcher in Jerusalem, fulfilling his final promise to his dead lord.

As the days passed, the sun grew even brighter, the sea even more blue. The Holy Land beckoned. They sailed beneath the dazzling white cliffs of the Greek islands and took on supplies at Cyprus. William gazed far across the water toward the rugged coastline of the mainland. He thought of those pilgrims who had made the treacherous journey to the East on foot, following the Rhine and Danube rivers through the dark forests of the Balkans. Every day they had faced death from starvation, wolves, or bandits. All to visit the Holy Land, to renew their faith. (continued on page 38)

(Above) As Crusaders prepare to depart for the Holy Land, their ships are loaded with horses, weapons and supplies. (Opposite) William Marshal sees the Holy Land for the first time.

The Crusades

For Christians in medieval Europe, Jerusalem was a Holy City and a magnet for pilgrims. But during the late eleventh century, the Muslim Turks who had conquered the area began imprisoning and enslaving visitors. Pope Urban II called for a crusade, or holy war, to push out the "Muslim infidels." For the next two centuries, knights from every kingdom in Europe headed east under the banner of the Crusader's cross and invaded the Holy Land repeatedly. The First Crusade, launched in 1095, proved victorious four years later when the Crusaders took the Holy City and established the Kingdom of Jerusalem to govern the Holy Land. Their victory was short-lived, however, and the Turks quickly won back part of what they had lost. The Second Crusade in 1147 failed to dislodge them. In 1187, Saladin, the great Muslim warrior, reconquered Jerusalem. Several more crusades followed, including two disastrous ventures made up almost entirely of children. Crusaders built castles and controlled parts of the Holy Land for many years, but never really broke the Muslim hold on the Holy City. By 1291 the last of the Crusaders had abandoned their cause and set sail for home.

(Left) Pope Urban II calls for a crusade to reclaim the Holy Land. (Top) A fifteenth-century depiction of the siege of Antioch. (Above left) During the siege of Nicea, Crusaders catapulted human heads over the city wall. (Above right) Crusaders arriving on the shores of the Holy Land.

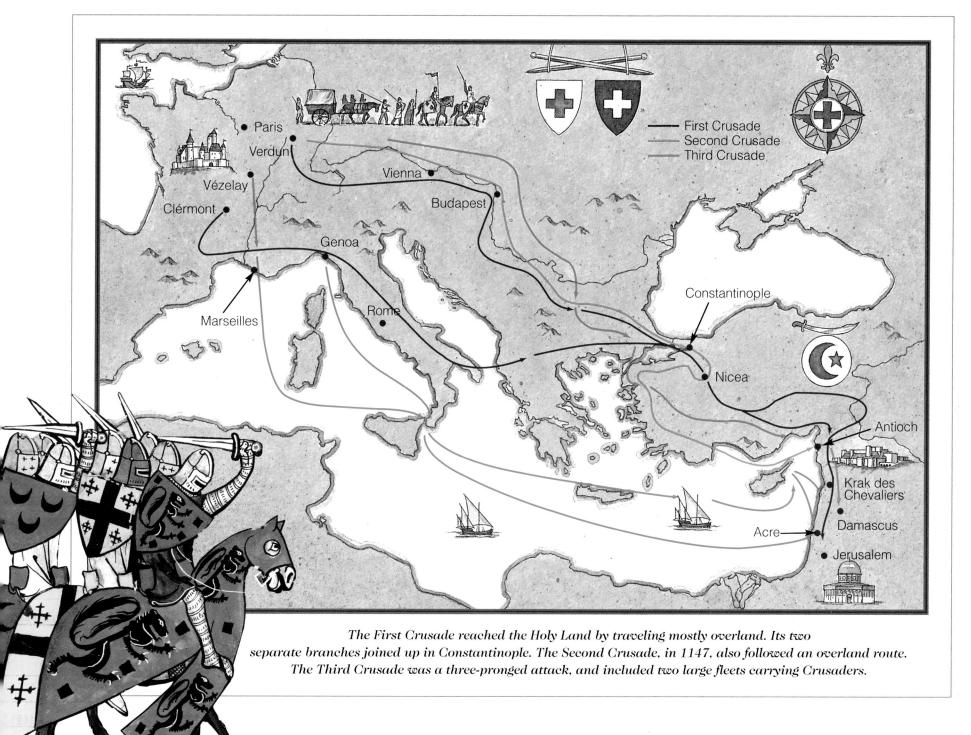

First Crusade
Second Crusade
Third Crusade

Paris
Verdun
Vézelay
Clérmont
Vienna
Budapest
Genoa
Marseilles
Rome
Constantinople
Nicea
Antioch
Krak des Chevaliers
Acre
Damascus
Jerusalem

The First Crusade reached the Holy Land by traveling mostly overland. Its two separate branches joined up in Constantinople. The Second Crusade, in 1147, also followed an overland route. The Third Crusade was a three-pronged attack, and included two large fleets carrying Crusaders.

After taking Jerusalem in 1089, the victorious Crusaders looted it of treasure. In this illustration from a later account of the crusades, they are shown piling up their booty outside the city walls.

Jerusalem, Christians had come here to fight the Turks for control of the Holy Land. Although the mighty Muslim leader Saladin had recently agreed to a temporary truce, reminders of the war were everywhere.

William had seen plenty of bloodshed and misery in his time, but nothing like this. The roadside was littered with the skeletons of horses, oxen, and men. Many were already bleached white by the sun. Others were still being picked over by crows and looters. He saw the remains of a wagon with its wheels buried up to the hubs — abandoned during the winter rains that turned the land into a sea of mud every year. He saw starving families dressed in rags, chewing on fig leaves for nourishment. He watched one man kill another over a few green lemons. He saw lepers with missing ears and noses, people with no legs. He saw slave trains and children traveling alone, pawing at strangers for food like animals.

Yet alongside this suffering and poverty was wealth such as he had never imagined. There were camels and wagons laden with goods for trade: silks dyed brilliant shades of red and blue,

(continued from page 34) The road from Acre to Jerusalem was dusty and hot. The old Roman stones were rough and cracked from the passage of thousands of pilgrims and soldiers. For more than eighty years, since the first European knights had taken

The Knights Templar

The Order of Knights Templar, founded in Jerusalem around 1120, was originally formed to protect pilgrims on their way to the Holy City. Later, its members guarded much of the Holy Land. In many ways, the Templars resembled monks. Like monks, the young knights wishing to join this sacred order had to believe in the Christian faith and could not marry. They also spent much of their time in prayer. In battle, however, the Templars — garbed in white tunics emblazoned with a red cross — struck terror in the hearts of their enemies. At its peak, the Order boasted more than 20,000 fearless members (perhaps William Marshal among them) and was supported by gifts of lands and money from the nobility.

By 1291, with the final conquest of the Holy Land by the Muslims, the Order no longer had a purpose and was in a slow decline. In 1307, King Philip VI of France, jealous of the power and wealth of the Knights Templar in his country, seized their lands and imprisoned their members. He accused the Templars of heresy and prevailed upon the Pope to confiscate all lands throughout Europe belonging to the Order. Finally, in 1314, Philip had its leaders burned at the stake.

(Left) This twelfth-century image showing a Templar knight riding into battle is from a chapel belonging to the Order. (Above) By order of King Philip VI of France, the Templars' leaders are burned at the stake.

impossibly soft carpets, olive oils, wines, and fruits. He saw horses that could only have come from heaven itself. The long-legged, high-stepping Arabian mares wore silver shoes and intricately tooled leather saddles finer than anything he had seen in the richest courts of Europe.

Outside Arsuf, the road looked like a carnival, with acrobats, musicians, and traders selling glass beads, copper kettles, and ivory. One man approached every traveler with a pouch that he claimed held the true bones of Christ. A man in a turban flashed a steel sword that cut through silk as easily as air. Its blade, sharpened to a hair's breadth, seemed to ripple like water.

And through it all the sun beat down. William wiped the sweat from his eyes. He tried to imagine what it would be like to be dressed in full mail and helmet, trapped between the blistering sand and the scorching sun. How did men fight in this heat? How did a man find the strength to raise his sword?

One afternoon at a river crossing, he came upon a thief. The man was dressed in rags, riding a half-starved nag. He was hurriedly emptying the pack of a horse tethered by the side of the road. William saw him take a purse of coins, a water pouch, gloves, a knife. The owner of the horse was nowhere to be seen.

Saladin, the great Muslim military leader, succeeded in taking Jerusalem from the Crusaders in 1187. In 1189, he defeated the Third Crusade, which was sent to win it back.

William prepared to pass by. If it had been his horse, that man would be missing an eye, or worse. But the road to Jerusalem was thick with thieves. He had seen dozens of such incidents.

The horse's owner seemed to appear from nowhere. He wore a white tunic with a red cross stitched to the shoulder. A Templar knight, William saw, fighting in the name of God. But a warrior just the same.

The thief paled as the knight held his sword to the man's throat.

"By the legs of God, do not kill me!" the man begged. William waited for the knight to run the man through or at least kill his horse. Instead, to his amazement, the Templar held out his hand and pulled the man to his feet. Then he handed him his water pouch and calmly watched as the thief hurriedly rode away.

At last William reached the east wall of Jerusalem. Here and there workmen on ladders and scaffolds repaired the crumbling walls of the Holy City. He noticed that rich and poor had stopped to bathe before passing through the Golden Gate. Their turbans and simple flowing robes looked cool and clean.

Inside the stone walls, Jerusalem gleamed. The round

Krak des Chevaliers Castle

Once the Holy Land had been captured, the Crusader knights busied themselves building castles to defend it. Perhaps the greatest of these was Krak des Chevaliers (the name, meaning Knight's Castle, is a mixture of French and Arabic). Situated high on a hill in Syria, it guarded the northern approach to Jerusalem. Begun in 1142 by the Knights Hospitaler, the other great order of Crusader knights, the castle boasted both inner and outer walls, separated by a wide moat. There was room for 2,000 men inside. After Jerusalem fell, the Hospitalers continued to hold it until 1271.

(Above) Krak des Chevaliers as it looks today.
(Below) The castle's twin set of walls provided superb defense.

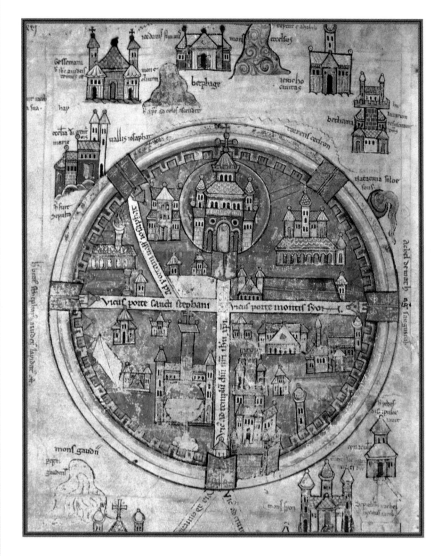

(Above) A map of Jerusalem from Crusader times prominently shows the Church of the Holy Sepulcher. Built on what was believed to be the site of Jesus' tomb, it was regarded as one of Christianity's holiest spots. (Opposite) William lays Prince Henry's robe before the altar at the Church of the Holy Sepulcher. To pray at this church was the goal of every Crusader knight.

Dome of the Rock rose above the flat rooftops of the houses. The streets were filled with the scents of pepper, cloves, and lemons. The sound of a tambourine drifted from a nearby alley.

William walked across the stone courtyard to the pink walls of the Church of the Holy Sepulcher. Inside, it was cool. His footsteps echoed on the mosaic floor. Above him, light streamed through the high windows.

William approached the steps of the shrine that held the tomb of Christ. He knelt, kissed the prince's robe and laid it on the steps. Poor young Henry. William had taught him the knightly skills, but he had failed to teach him the most important lesson: a knight with no one to serve but himself was no knight at all.

William bent his head and prayed. He remembered his hasty knighting ceremony twenty years before. He had felt nothing then but the urge to spur his horse onto the battlefield, to wield his sword, to bring down the enemy and win.

Now he knew that bravery in battle was not the same as bravery of spirit. Skill, courage, and loyalty were nothing without humility, without generosity, without the knowledge that one was serving a higher good.

William rose slowly to his feet. He was almost forty years old, and his back hurt. He would return to England and serve his God and his king as best he could. Perhaps he would marry, pass on his name to sons of his own.

And the next time he unseated the enemy, he would give him back his horse and offer him a hand to help him to his feet.

Epilogue

By the time William Marshal returned from the Holy Land in 1187, his prime fighting days were over. But the knightly qualities of loyalty and service continued to guide him for the rest of his life. In 1190, Richard the Lion-Heart, Henry II's son and successor, embarked on the Third

Crusade to retake Jerusalem. Richard chose William Marshal — the most loyal man he knew — to help manage his kingdom in his absence.

William Marshal devoted the rest of his life to the service of the English kings. In exchange, he was granted the hand of Isabel, the Countess of Pembroke, one of the richest heiresses in England. The match gave him control of lands and castles in England, Ireland, Normandy, and Wales and

(Below) Pembroke Castle in Wales. Originally a stockade of logs and earth, it was transformed by William into a mighty stone fortress when he became Earl of Pembroke. (Right) Shown here are the four kings William Marshal served: Henry II, Richard I, John I and Henry III.

made him one of the most powerful barons in the land.

Richard's brother and successor, King John, died in 1216, leaving the throne to his son, nine-year-old Henry III. William Marshal was chosen to be regent, in charge of running the country until the king came of age. He knighted the boy himself and, over the next two years, helped bring stability to England. He negotiated a peace treaty between England and France, replenished the empty royal treasury, and gained honors for himself and his family.

The end came when he was seventy-two years old, an astonishing age for those times, especially for a man who had spent much of his life risking life and limb. For three months he lay sick and dying in his manor at Caversham, watched over night and day by his family and knights. During those months, he made provisions for the future of each one of his ten children, including

This effigy of William Marshal, Earl of Pembroke, graces his tomb in London's Temple Church, originally a chapel of the Knights Templar.

his five daughters and his youngest sons. Before he died on May 14, 1219, he asked that his body be covered with two silk cloths that he had brought from the Holy Land thirty years before.

After his death, William Marshal's eldest son hired a poet to write about the life of his remarkable father. The resulting poem, written in French, was more than 19,000 lines long. It has come down to us as one of the earliest biographies of a person who was not a king, and it gives a detailed, vivid picture of a real knight's life in the Middle Ages.

On the day of William Marshal's funeral, food, drink, shoes, and clothing were distributed to the poor, as he had requested. At his burial, the Archbishop of Canterbury proclaimed Marshal to be "the best knight who ever lived." He was, all agreed, a man who truly embodied the knightly virtues of skill at arms, courage, loyalty, and service.

Glossary

Constantinople: The old name for what is today the city of Istanbul.

Destrier: A strong, powerful warhorse ridden by a knight.

Duchy: Usually a subdivision of a larger country, ruled over by a duke or duchess.

Hauberk: The main part of a knight's armor. A coat made of mail.

Heresy: A religious belief disapproved of by the church.

Infidel: One outside the Christian religion. In the Middle Ages, Muslims were regarded as infidels.

Mail: Often incorrectly called chain mail, mail was a knight's armor, created by joining together thousands of metal links.

Melée: A battle fought between two groups of knights at a tournament.

Palfrey: A knight's horse used for transportation, not war.

Quintain: A dummy that knights used for practice, charging it with their lances on horseback.

Tilting: Combat between two knights using lances, separated by a "tilt," or barrier.

Troubadours: Popular singers or reciters of poems and songs about love.

Picture Credits

Index

Acknowledgments

The events of this story, including portions
of dialogue, are based on *L'Historie de Guillaume le
Maréchal* (ca. 1228) and on several scholarly
works written about that text.

Madison Press Books would especially like to
thank our historical adviser, K. Corey Keeble
of the Royal Ontario Museum.

Design and Art Direction:
Gordon Sibley Design Inc.

Editorial Director:
Hugh M. Brewster

Project Editor:
Ian R. Coutts

Editorial Assistance:
Susan Aihoshi

Production Director:
Susan Barrable

Production Co-ordinator:
Donna Chong

Maps:
Jack McMaster

Color Separation:
Colour Technologies

Printing and Binding:
TWP Singapore

IN THE TIME OF KNIGHTS
was produced by
Madison Press Books,
which is under the direction
of Albert E. Cummings

Recommended Further Reading

Medieval Knights
by Trevor Cairns
*(Cambridge University
Press)*

A portait of knighthood
from its origins and glory
days to its decline and
final demise.

Days of the Knights
by Christopher Maynard
*(Fenn, Canada) (Dorling
Kindersley, U.S.)*

With many photographs
and illustrations, this book
describes day-to-day life
in the Middle Ages.

Castles
by Philip Steele
(Kingfisher)

A description of life within
castle walls including what
it was like when a castle
was under siege.

Knights
by Andrea Hopkins
(Shooting Star Press)

An illustrated volume
covers all the elements of
a knightly life — in war
and in peace (adult
reading level).